Edward Arber, John Udall

The state of the Church of England laid open in a conference

between Diotrephes a bishop and Paul a preacher of the

word of God

Edward Arber, John Udall

The state of the Church of England laid open in a conference between Diotrephes a bishop and Paul a preacher of the word of God

ISBN/EAN: 9783337200855

Printed in Europe, USA, Canada, Australia, Japan

Cover: Foto ©Lupo / pixelio.de

More available books at **www.hansebooks.com**

The English Scholar's Library of Old and Modern Works

REV. JOHN UDALL

The

State of the Church of England

laid open in a Conference between DIOTREPHES
a Bishop, TERTULLUS a Papist, DEMETRIUS
a Usurer, PANDOCHUS an Innkeeper, and
PAUL a Preacher of the word of GOD

[April 1588]

EDITED BY

EDWARD ARBER

F.S.A. ETC. LATE EXAMINER IN ENGLISH
LANGUAGE AND LITERATURE
TO THE UNIVERSITY OF
LONDON

WESTMINSTER

ARCHIBALD CONSTABLE AND CO.

1895

CONTENTS.

৯ৼৎ

For Speakers, see title page at p. 1.

₊ The Scene of the Dialogue is in PANDOCHUS's Inn which is in
a posting town, apparently in the North of England, on
the high road from London to Edinburgh.

BIBLIOGRAPHY.

For a list of the principal works up to 1606, on both sides of this Controversy, see PETER
FAIRLAMBE, *The Recantation of a Brownist Or a Reformed Puritan.* 1606. 4to.

I. SOME ANTECEDENT ENGLISH WORKS IN THIS CONTROVERSY.

[With Press Marks of some copies in the British Museum.]

1574.

[WALTER TRAVERS] A full and plaine declaration of Ecclesiasticall Discipline owt off the word of
God, and off the declininge off the churche of England from the same. Imprinted [*evidently
abroad*] M.D.LXXIIII. [3932. e.]   See *p.* 9.

1575.

THOMAS CARTWRIGHT's *Second Reply* to Dr. WHITGIFT's *Second Answer.*
[?] The History of the Troubles at Frankfort.

1577.

THOMAS CARTWRIGHT. *The rest of the Second Reply* to Dr. WHITGIFT's *Second Answer.*
                                                              See *p.* 10.

1582.

[ROBERT BROWN, *the* Brownist.] A book which sheweth the life and manners of all true
Christians. Middleburg. [*Two copies are in Lambeth Library.*]

1583.

[?] An Abstract, of certaine Acts of Parliament : of certaine her Maiesties Iniunctions [697. f. 2'1] :
usually referred to as the *Abstract.* There were two undated editions. One in black letter
without pagination [697. f. 2/1] : the other in Roman letter and paged. [697. f. 15.] [See *p.* 12.]

1584.

[RICHARD COSIN.] An Answer to the two first and principall Treatises of a certeine factious libell,
put foorth latelie, without name of Author or Printer, and without approbation by authoritie,
vnder the title of *An Abstract &c.* [697. f. 2/2].
*[DUDLEY FENNER, Minister at Middleburgh.] A Counter Poyson modestly written for the time,
to make answere to the obiections and reproches, wherewith the *aunswerer* to the *Abstract,*
would disgrace the holy Discipline of Christ. [1360. a.]   See *p.* 9.
[?] A Fruitefull Sermon, vpon the 3. 4. 5. 6. 7. and 8. verses, of the 12. Chapiter of the Epistle
of S. *Paul* to the *Romans,* very necessary for these times to be read of all men, for their further
instruction and edification, in things concerning their faith and obedience to saluation. [C. 46.
a/2.] Printed by WALDEGRAVE.   See *p.* 9.
[?] A Briefe and plaine declaration, concerning the desires of those faithfull Ministers, that haue
and do seeke for the Discipline and reformation of the Church of Englande : Which may serue
for a just Apologie, against the false accusations and slaunders of their aduersaries. [C. 46. a 1.]
Printed by WALDEGRAVE. *This work is usually referred to (from its headline) as* A learned
Discourse of Ecclesiasticall Gouernment.   See *p.* 9.

1585.

[?] A Lamentable Complaint of the Commonalty, By Way Of Suppl'cation To The High Court
Of Parliament, For A Learned Ministery. In Anno 1585. [4103. b.]
*[?] The Vnlawful Practises Of Prelates Against Godly Ministers, The Maintainers Of The
Discipline Of God. [111. a. 8.]
*[?] The Judgment of a most reuerend and learned Man from beyond sees, concerning a threefold
order of Bishops (*i.e. of God, of man, and of the Devil.*) [Not seen. See HERBERT's AMES'S
Typ. Ant. p. 1654. *Ed.* 1790.
    ∵ *For printing these last three tracts,* WALDEGRAVE *is imprisoned, see p.* xi.

   * These works are reprinted in *A Parte of a register &c.* [Edinburgh 1593.] [697. f. 14.]

II. DIOTREPHES.

ISSUES IN THE AUTHOR'S LIFETIME.

As a separate publication.

1. [April 1588. London. 8vo.] See title on *p.* 1.

ISSUES SINCE HIS DEATH.

As a separate publication.

2. 15 April 1879. Southgate, London, N. 8vo. The present impression.

INTRODUCTION.

HIS satirical Dialogue, quoted for shortness at the time as *DIOTREPHES*, was written against the administration of the Anglican Bishops, by the Rev. JOHN UDALL, the Preacher at Kingston upon Thames; and was printed to his utter ruin, by ROBERT WALDEGRAVE, the Puritan printer and publisher living at this date outside Temple Bar.

WALDEGRAVE was a Worcestershire man, as is proved by the entry of his apprenticeship in the Stationers' *Registers*—

GREFFETH ROBERTE WALGRAVE the sonne of RYCHARD WALGRAVE late of BLACKLAY in the Countye of Worcestre yeoman Deceassed hath put hym self apprentes to WYLLIAM GREFFETH. Cetizan and stacioner of London / from the feaste of the nativite of saynte John bapteste [24 June] *anno* 1568 viij yeres   vjd.

Transcript &c., i. 372. *Ed.* 1875.

He would have been entitled to his freedom of the Company in the summer of 1576; but as the *Register* for that year has long been lost, there is no precise record of the date from which he would be entitled to publish a book in London.

He had in 1588, been actually publishing works, chiefly religious, for some ten years past: and—especially since the advent of WHITGIFT to the Primacy—had suffered many things at the hands of the Bishops, of some which *MARTIN MARPRELATE* has preserved to us the following accounts—

Which Harmonie / was translated and printed by that puritan Cambridg printer / Thomas Thomas. And although

the booke came out by publike authoritie / yet by your leaue
the Bishops haue called them in / as things against their
state. And trust me / his grace will owe that puritane
printer as good a turne / as hee paid vnto Robert Walde-
graue for his sawcines / in printing my frend and deare
brother Diotrephes his Dialogue. Well frend Thomas I
warne you before hand / look to your selfe.—*The Epistle* [*Nov.*
1588], *p.* 8. *Ed.* 1879.

Pitifully complayning / is there any reason (my Lords grace)
why knaue Thackwell the printer / which printed popishe
and trayterous welshe bookes in wales / shoulde haue more
fauour at your gracelesse handes / then poore Walde-graue /
who neuer printed book against you / that contayneth
eyther treason or impietie. Thackwell is at libertie to walke
where he will / and permitted to make the most he could of
his presse and letters : whereas Robert Walde-graue dares
not shew his face for the bloodthirstie desire you haue for
his life / onely for printing of bookes which toucheth the
bishops Myters. You know that Walde-graues printing
presse and Letters were takken away : his presse being
timber / was sawen and hewed in pieces / the yron work
battered and made vnseruiceable / his Letters melted / with
cases and other tooles defaced (by Iohn Woolfe / alias
Machiuill / Beadle of the Stationers / and most tormenting
executioner of Walde-graues goods) and he himselfe vtterly
deprived for euer [of] printing againe / hauing a wife and sixe
small children. Will this monstrous crueltie neuer bee
reuenged thinke you ? When Walde-graues goods was to be
spoiled and defaced / there were some printers / that rather
then all the goods should be spoyled / offered money for it /
towardes the reliefe of the mans wife and children / but this
coulde not be obtayned / and yet popishe Thackwell / though
hee printed popish and trayterous bookes / may haue the fauor to make money of his presse and letters. And reason to[o].
For Walde-graues profession ouerthroweth the popedome of
Lambehith / but Thackwels popery maintayneth the same.

And now that Walde-graue hath neither presse nor letters / his grace may dine and sup the quieter. But looke to it brother Canterburie / certainly without your repentance / I feare me / you shalbe *Hildebrand in deed. Walde-graue ^{A fyrebrana in deede.} hath left house and home / by reason of your vnnaturall tyrannie : hauing left behinde him a poore wife and sixe Orphanes / without any thing to relieue them. (For the husband you haue bereaued both of his trade and goods) Be you assured that the crie of these will one day preuaile against you / vnlesse you desist from persecuting.—*The Epistle, pp.* 22, 23.

Concerning Walde-graue / its no matter how you deal with him / heez a foolish fellow / to suffer you to spoyle his presse and letters : an a had bin my worships printer / ide a kept him from your clouches. And yet it is pitie to belye the diuell : and therefore you shall not belye / him and goe scotfree. As for the presse that Walde-graue solde / he did it by order / vz. He solde it to an allowed printer / I.C. one of his owne companie / with the knowledge of his Warden / Henry Denham / &c. And cal you this fauor / in releasing him after long imprisonment ? But I will give you a president of great fauor in deede / wherein you may see what an vngratefull fellow Walde-graue is to his grace / who hath bin so good vnto him from time [to] time. There being a controuersie betweene another printer and Walde-graue (all matters of printing being committed by the LL. of the Counsell to his grace) Walde-graue made one of his company his friende (who could do much with his grace) to deale for him / who brake the matter to his worship / being at Croydon in his Orcharde : so soone as the partie named Walde-graue / he sweetly aunswered him / saying : if it had bin any of the company saue him / he would haue graunted the suite / but in no case to Walde-graue. Well Walde-graue / obtayned the R[ight]. H[onorable] Lord Treasurers letter in his behalfe to his grace / who when he had read it / said / I will answer my L. Treasurer : with that Walde-graue intreated for his fauorable letter to the Wardens of his companie / which in the end through D. Coosins he obtained (though late) yet went home at night / thinking to deliuer it in the morning : but before he was ready / the Wardens were with him / and [ar]rested him with a Purciuant vpon his graces commandement / Walde-graue telling them there was a letter from his grace / which he received late the last night at Croidon : who answered / they knew it well inough / but this is his pleasure now : so they caried Walde-graue to prison / and in this / his grace was so good vnto him / as to help him with an hundred marks ouer the shulders. If this be your fauour / God keepe me from you / ka M. Marprelate. Bishops haue iustly received according to their desertes / hauing found greater fauour at my worships hands than euer they deserued / being notorious / disobedient and godlesse persons / vnthrifty spenders and consumers of the fruits / not of their own labors / (as you say Walde-graue was) but of the pos-sessions of the church / persons that haue violated their faith to god / his church / hir majesty / and this whol[e] kingdom / and wittingly bring vs al without the great mercy of god to our vndoing : so that our wiues / children and seruants / haue cause to curse al L. Bb. Lo *T.C.* you see that I haue a good gift in imitation / and me thinkes I have brought your wordes into a marueilous good sense / wher as before in the cause of Walde-graue / they were ilfauoredly wrested : and as for his wife and children / they haue iust cause to curse Iohn of London / and Iohn of Canterburie / for their tyranni-zing ouer him : by imprisoning and spoyling his goods / and vexing his poore wife and children / with continuall rifeling his house with their purciuants: who in Nouember [1588] last / violently rusht into his house / breaking through the maine wall thereof after midnight / taking away his goods / for some of the purciuants solde his books vp and downe the streats / to watchmen and others. Ah you Antichristian prelats / when will you make an ende of defending your tyrannie / by the blood and rapine of her maiesties subiectes ? You haue bin the consumers of the fruits of Walde-graues labors : for

[marginal note: A new reuenge for an old grudge.]

haue you not sent him so often to prison / that it seemed you made a common occupation thereof? For assoon as any book is printed in the defence of Christs holy discipline / or for ye detecting of your Antichristian dealings / but your rauening purciuantes flye citie and countrie to seeke for Walde-graue / as though he were bound by statute vnto you / either to make known who printed seditious books against my L. O the greatnes Face / or to go to prison himselfe / and threatned fauor. of his graces with the racke. And are you not ashamed to say / that he euer violated his fayth? you know wel inough / that he is neither Archb. nor L. B. The case thus stood / after he had remained a long time in prison / not that time when Hartwell his graces secretary wisht that his grace might neuer eat bit of bread after he released him. Nor at that time when you profane *T.C.* told him / that all puritans had traiterous hearts. Nor at that time Walde-graue tolde his grace / that he was worse than Bo͟n͟ner in regard of the time. Nor that time when he was straungely released by one of the Lorde of good Londons Swans. Neither was it at yat time / when his grace (good conscionable noble man) violated his promise / in that he told the wardens of the stacioners / that if Walde-graue woulde come quietly to him / and cease printing of seditious bookes / he would pardon what was past / and the wardens promised his wife / that if he were committed / they would lye at his graces gate til he were released / and for al this / yet he was committed to the white Lyon / where he laye sixe weekes. Nor it was not at that time / when his grace allowed Watson the purciuant / to take of Walde-graue / 13.s.4. pence / for cariyng of him to the white Lyon. But it was that time / when his grace kept him 20. weekes together in the white lyon / for printing the Complaint of the comminaltie / the Practize of prelats / A learned mans iudgment / &c. Means being vsed for his liberty / his frend who was bound for him told him / his liberty was obtained in maner following. You must be bounde saith he / in a 100. pounds / to print no more books hereafter / but such as shalbe authorized by hir Maiesty

or his grace / or such as were before lawfully authorized :
wherunto he answered / that it was not possible for him to
containe himselfe within the compasse of that bond / neither
Whereby it
may appeare
he swore not
to his friend. should his consent euer go to the same (the same
wil D. Coosins witnes (that maidenly Doctor / who
sits cheek by ioll with you) if he will speake a
trueth / which words Walde-graue vttered to him / going in
the old pallas at westminster with his keeper before he was
released) yet he woulde gladly haue his libertie if he might
lawfully. For saide he / I being a poore workeman to my
companie / cannot possibly obserue it. For many bookes
heretofore printed / had *cum priuilegio,* and yet were neuer
authorized : and againe / that it were but a folly for him to
sue to her Maiestie / the office were very base and vnfit for
her. And he might be wel assured that Caiphas of Cant.
would never authorize any thing for his behoofe / and so
it fell out. And thus Martin hath prooued you in this / as in
all other things / to be lyars. And what is it that you Bb.
and your hangones will not saye by Walde-graue / whom you ˙
would hang if you could.—*Hay any worke for Cooper* [23 *March,*
1589], *pp.* 43-46. *Ed.* 1880.

As we shall see in our *Introductory Sketch &c.,* that it was WALDE-
GRAVE himself that set up in type these different accounts of his maltreat-
ment, as parts of these two Martinist productions printed by him at the
wandering secret press ; we cannot but regard them as his personal con-
tribution to the Controversy.

II.

THE process of WALDEGRAVE's ruination is thus officially
described in the *Records* of the Stationers' Company—

May 13, 1588. Whereas Master COLDOCK
Warden, THOMAS WOODCOCK, OLIVER WILKES, and
JOHN WOLF, on the 16 of April last, vpon search of
ROBERT WAL[DE]GRAUES house, did seise of his and bring to
Stationers hall, according to the late decrees of the Starre-

chamber, and by vertue thereof A presse with twoo paire of cases, with certaine Pica Romane, and Pica Italian letters, with diuers books entituled: *The state of the Churche of England laid open &c.* For that the said WAL[DE]GRAVE without aucthority, and contrary to the said Decrees had printed the said book. Yt is now in full court—ordered and agreed by force of the said decrees, and according to the same, That the said books shall be burnte, and the said presse, letters and printing stuffe defaced and made vnserviceable.

W. HERBERT's Edition of AMES's *Typ. Ant.,* ii. 1145. *Ed.* 1786.

In the Stationers' *Registers* at this date also occur the following entries—·

Item   Delyvered to JOHN WOLF the xvj[th] day of Apryll [1588] to goe to Croydon to my Lordes grace about WAL[DE]GRAVE   iiij[s] /

for breakinge a presse and meltinge of letters . . . xij[d] /

Transcript, i. 528. *Ed.* 1875.

Strangely enough, in another part of the *Registers* occurs the following entry on the very day of the promulgation of the above decision—

13 *Maii* [1588].

ROBERTE   A copie whereof he is to bring the title   vj[d]
WAL[DE]GRAVE   *Transcript,* ii. 490. *Ed.* 1875.

This title he never did bring : but disappears from all avowed printing from this date until March 1590, when he is established in Edinburgh as the Royal Printer for Scotland ; from which country he did not return till the accession of JAMES I. to the English throne.

III.

THIS *Dialogue* — which also helped to bring about JOHN UDALL's premature death—is but a brief, yet quietly sarcastic statement of the general social War between the Bishops and the Presbyters in England, which will be more fully noticed in our *Introductory Sketch &c.* ; and in respect to its effects on UDALL himself, in our reprint of his *Demonstration of Discipline.*

There are some striking points incidentally touched upon in this tract. It is an additional confirmation, if any were wanted, of Lord BURLEIGH's

Execution of Justice in England, that there had not been even a slight casual persecution of Roman Catholic Englishmen, *as Roman Catholics,* under Queen ELIZABETH ; as there had been of Protestants, under her sister MARY.

It is a testimony to the rapid growth of Puritanism in the four years that had now elapsed since WHITGIFT's advance to the Primacy, and so is another evidence of the utter futility of a policy of repression in matters of religious belief.

The stolid obduracy of the Bishops, their utter unwillingness to make the least concession, and so to satisfy moderate men ; that significant absence in them of least movement for reform in Parliament, which drew on them the censure of Lord BACON in his *Advertisement,* is also clearly brought out in this, the forerunning tract of the *MARTIN MARPRELATE* Controversy.

The strong delusion in all the religious teachers of the time—Protestant as well as Puritan — that the Lending of Money at Interest was a sin, is depicted in the character of **Demetrius.** It was not (as may be seen in Lord BACON's Essay on *Usury,* 1626) till another generation had passed away, that Political Economy, aided by the growing surplus wealth of the nation, overcame this vulgar error, which sprang from a confusing of things human and divine.

Lastly, we may note, the vast influence which the mind of CALVIN still exercised on the faith of millions : so that to differ from his views, was thought to be a departing from GOD. This comes out clearly in the following attack on the " freewil men ; " that is, on the Arminians before ARMINIUS.

Diotrep. Doe you not also like of the preaching of predestination ?

Paul Yea, or els should I dislike of preaching the trueth, for it is a part of Gods reuealed will.

Diotreph So do not I in these daies, when there be so manye weake ones, I thinke it to be a very break-necke of all religion.

Paul I haue heard of freewil men that haue saide so, but I neuer heard [a] man of learning affirme it, but one that was a byshoppe in a Sermon, but his wordes were no lesse than blasphemie, and so are yours, and al they that say or think the same are guiltie of no lesse sinne.—*pp.* 14-15.

Altogether, while written with a quietude of expression which must have been difficult to the writer, this *Conference* is as vigorous a bit of Puritanism as anything that has come down to us from that age.

The state of the Church of

Englande, laide open in a conference
betweene *Diotrephes* a Byshopp, *Tertullus* a
Papiste, *Demetrius* an vsurer, *Pandochus* an
Inne-keeper, and *Paule* a preacher of the
worde of God.

PSAL. 122. 6.

*Pray for the peace of Hierusalem, let them
prosper that loue thee.*

REVEL. 14.9 10.

*And the third Angel folowed them, saying
with a loud voice, if any man worship the
beast and his image, and receiue his marke in
his forhead, or on his hand, the same shall
drinke of the wine of the wrath of God.*

THE PRÆFACE.

Entle Reader, I haue sette down here in a Dialog, the practize of Satan which he vseth (as I haue obserued by experience) to subuert and vtterly ouerturne the course of the Gospel here in England; the names of the speakers, containe in them for the most part, the matter that they defend, and the affection that they are of. For thou knowest that *Diotrephes* was he of whom S. Iohn speaketh in his third Epistle, verse 9. that louing to haue the preheminence, disturbed the course of good things in the Church, and therfore sustaineth the person of a Byshopp, or Byshoply prelate. *Tertullus* is he of whom Luke speaketh in the 24. Acts, that was the speaker in the ambassage from Ierusalem to Fœlix the gouerner, against *Paule*, in the defence of ceremonies abrogated, for the ouerthrowe of the Gospel, and so representeth the papists, that maintaine their traish, to the rooting out of true religion. *Demetrius* is he of whom mention is made, in Actes 19. that was enemie to *Paule*, because he liued by an vnlawfull trade, and for that cause doth play the part of an vserer. *Paule* was the defender, you knowe of the Gospel in sinceritie, and he whose pen the holy Ghost did vse to expresse the discipline of the church most clerely, and therefore speaketh for the ministers of our time, that stand for reformation. *Pandochus* is an In-keeper in Greeke, and it is as much as to saye, a recciuer of all, and a soother of euerye man for his gaine ; so that the persons in their nature thus considered : it remaineth that thou wouldest be intreated by me, whosoeuer thou art, to whom this little booke shall come, that thou wouldest in reading of it, set al affection aside, and neither belieue it, because on[e] of thy disposition did pen it, neither yet reiect it, because it was not composed by one of thy complexion; but consider well of the speeches vttered by euery partie, and compare them with the practize of the worlde, and then looke what it is, that so hardeneth Pandochus in atheism, Demetrius in vsery, and Tertullus in papistrie; and you shall (I doubt not) plainly perceiue, that the cause of all vngodlines so to raigne in euery place, and of the papists so to increase in strength and number, ariseth from our byshops and their vnlawfull gouernement; on the other side, look into the answers that Diotrephes maketh to Paul, and the counsel that Tertullus giueth to Diotrephes, and compare them with the practize of the B. in all poyntes, and you shall euidently perceiue that the cause why the gospel beeing so longe preached, hath taken so little root, ariseth from them onely, forsomuch as they haue weakened the knees of the true preachers, and euery way crossed them in all good actions. I haue touched thinges verie briefely of purpose, partly for that they who see what reformation meaneth, wil quickly vnderstand my meaning, and partly for that I would haue him that vnderstandeth not mine intent and would be resolued, to confer at large of it with some godly learned of his further instruction. Now I pray thee, let me intreat thee to think thus of mine intent; namely, that it is not of purpose to disgrace any man, albeit we ought to disgrace them, by whom the sonn of God is disgraced: but especially to this end, that euery man in his calling, might see howe he is or hath beene made an instrument to do harme, or for want either of knowledge, or prouident forecast, being ouertaken vnder collour of right and law, and lastly that we all seing the subtleties of the deuill against the kingdom of Christ Iesus, may first of al returne to God by speedy repentance, from the wickednes that wee haue in our hands, which in deede is the cause of this curse vpon vs; and then praye vnto his Maiestie, that he would detect the craftie subtilties of all his aduersaries, reueale the trueth to those that are seduced and abused, and erect the kingdome of his sonne Christ Iesus amongst vs, by the forme of that discipline that his owne worde expresseth vnto vs.

Diotr Ine hoste, I pray you staye with me and my friende M[aster]. Tertullus, and tell vs some newes, for wee are lately come out of Scotland, and would heere before wee com nere London, in what state things doe stande, lest we comming on a sudden, speede as ill as we did at Edenborough, and S. Andrewes.

Pandoch Good my Lorde, I can tell you no great newes, for I go not so farre as to Church once in a moneth, but if I doe happen to go, one of my seruants doth come for me in all haste, to make merrie with one gueste or other, but there bee two in this house, that came from London, if it please your L[ordship]. I wil intreat one of them to come vnto you, it may be he can tell you some thing.

Diotr I pray thee doe so? you are welcome my friend, I vnderstand that you came from London, I pray you tell me some newes, for I hauing bene in Scotlande some space, haue not hearde muche of the state of England.

Demet My L[ord]. I heare no newes, but that our byshoppes (Gods blessing haue their harts for it) say prettie well, by one and by one, to these precise and hot preachers, for some of them are put to silence, some of them close prisoners in the Gate-house, some wel loaden with yrons in the White-lyon, and some in the Clinke, I hope to see them one day all put downe, for they trouble the whole land, and are neither contented to obey the authority of these holy fathers, neither yet will suffer vs to liue as our fore-fathers haue done before

2 *

vs, and here is a good fellowe, which I met yesterday vpon the way, who is iust of their opinion.

Pandoch I know not what religion he of whom you speake is of, but I am sure that hee hath many of our preachers quallities, for which I like him the wors[e], for since our preacher came, I haue not gained halfe so much as heretofore I did, but if I had but euerye night suche a guest, within one moneth all men would refraine from comming to mine house, and so I might beg.

Diotre Why mine hoste, what are his quallities, that you dislike so much?

Pandoch What? I will tell you, as soone as euer he lighted, my man that tooke his horse, chanced but to sweare by God, and he was reproouing of him by and by, and a gentleman cannot come all this euening, in any place where he is, but he is finding faut with him for one thing or another: and when he should go to supper with other gentlemen, sitting at the lower ende of the table, he would needs saye grace (forsooth) before and after supper, and so stay them that were hungrie, from their meat the longer, and from their sleepe afterward: but one wiser then the rest, serued him in his kind, for he started vp, saying my father had no grace before me, neither wil I haue any.

Diotr. I perceiue he is one of these peeuish Puritanes, that troubled the Churche, when my friend and I went into Scotland, haue not the bishops yet suppressed them, neither by countenance, nor by authoritie?

Tertul Suppressed? No my Lord, a friende of mine writt vnto mee, that one of theyr Preachers said in a pulpit, hee was perswaded that there were 10000. of them in Englande, and that the number of them encreased daily in euerie place of all estates and degrees.

Diotreph I am sorie for that, I maruel that you neuer told me of it?

Tertul I did of purpose conceale it, least, together with your ill successe that you, and so consequently I, had in Scotland, your griefe should haue bene agrauated, for I know how that the growing of them doth grieue you.

Diotr. You may be sure that it would haue grieued me, if you had tolde mee that, when you tolde mee of the increasing of your friendes the papistes, I thinke I should haue died for sorow.

Tertul I knowe that, therefore did I keepe it cloase, but if newes had come in like manner, of the growing of the Catholique religion vnto your man, that puritane knaue, hee would haue tolde it you at the firste, and so haue molested you the more.

Diotre You say well, and I perceiue it is better to haue a papist, then a puritane in an house, and more charitie to doe for them.

Pandoch Your Lorshippe asked me for some newes, but your speeche of your being and ill successe that you hadd in Scotland, giueth me occasion, to enquire of you (if I may bee so bolde) some Scottish newes.

Diotr. Ah my hoste, though it grieue mee to thinke vpon it, yet it easeth my stomacke to tell it. The puritanes in Scotland, hadd got vp their discipline, and vtterly ouerthrowen all the soueraigntie of byshopps, by which they preuailed so mightilie, that wee feared our fall in England shortly to ensue, wherevpon I was sent together with this my friend, who came out of Fraunce into England, to goe and seeke the subuersion of their generall assemblies, and the rest of their iurisdiction, wherein I preuailed a while, but now it is worse, then euer it was.

Pandoch How came it to passe, that when you had gotten some ground, you helde it not ?

Diotr Because the whole land cried out for Discipline againe, and the noble men so stiffely did stand to it ; and lastly, the Ministers that came home from England, dealte so boldly with the king that I was vtterly cast out wythout all hope, euer to do any good there again, and nowe I make homewarde in haste, least I loose all there also, but I praye you helpe me to speake with that puritane, I shall learne more by him, because he is better acquainted with the cause then eyther of you.

Demetri Hee may soone knowe more in that case then I, for I promise you, mine onely studie is in my counting house, to see my money, and when eache parcell is due vnto me.

Pandoch And I meddle with nothing but my In-keeping, as for these controuersies and this Scripturing, I neuer trouble my selfe with it, but I will go to him to see whether I can get him to come to your Lordship, but before I goe, I must beseech you to saye nothing to him as from me, for you know, I must be frendly to all, least I leese my custome, and driue away some of my guests.

Diotr. Great reason, for euerie man muste liue of his trade, neither must you tell him what I am.

Pandoch Sir, heere bee certaine gentlemen in another chamber, that hering of your comming from London, would gladly speake with you.

Paul Whence are they, can you tell?

Pandoch They are English men, but they are new come out of Scotland.

Paul I am willing to goe to them, though it be late, and so much the rather, because I long to heare some good news from thence.

Pandoch Here is the Gentleman that you desired to speake withall.

Diotre You are welcom my friend, I was desirous to speak with you for that I perceiue you came from London, I praye you can you tell vs any good newes?

Paul No surely, for I am a verie ill obseruer of such things.

Diotr. You seeme to be a minister, can you tell me what good successe my Lordes the bishops haue in their proceedings?

Paul They haue too good successe, they wax worse and worse, they growe euen to the heigth of their iniquity, so that I hope their kingdom wil not stand long?

Diotr. Why sir: what do they, that they offend you so grieuously?

Paule They stop the mouth of the sheepeheards, and set at libertie the rauening wolues, and turne the foxes among the lambes.

Diotr I muste desire you to expresse youre minde more plainely, for you seeme to bee so possessed with discontentment that it maketh you to speak (as it were) snatchingly?

Paul I confesse my selfe discontented, and greatly grieued, but yet not so much, as to make me lesse able to expresse my minde.

Diotr. I pray you therefore, laye open your former speches that I may vnderstand your meaning?

Paul My meaning is this, there are three abhominations committed by them : The firste is, that they doe beare suche an enimitie against the kingdome of Iesus Christe, that they put to silence one after another, and will neuer cease (if God bridle them not) vntill they haue rooted out of the Church, al the learned, godly, and painfull teachers : The second is, that they enlarge the libertie of the common enemies the papists : The last is, that they commit the feeding of the flockes of Christe, vnto those that prey vpon them, and either cannot, or will not labour to reclaime the wandering sheepe. So that the conclusion that may bee gathered vppon their actions, must needes be the euersion and ouerthrow of the gospell, and so consequently the bringing in of popery and atheisme.

Diotr. They put none to silence, but the puritans, who do in deed more hurt then good.

Paul I know no puritanes, if there be any, it is meete that they be put to silence, But Sathan taught the papistes, so too name the ministers of the Gospell, and you are his instrument in continuinge the same terme.

Diotr. I meane them, that are not contented with the state, but mislike the gouernment of the Churche, and woulde haue a newe forme of gouernement, which would marre all.

Paul Woulde you haue them contented with Anti-christian prelates, to be rulers of the spouse of Christ, when as the word of God hath prescribed expresly, another form direct contrary to that ?

Diotre I am a doctor of diuinitie at the lest, and yet coulde I neuer read any thinge in the worde of God, contrarie to this gouernement, neither yet to speake of any other, but that the ordering of the Churche is left to the discretion of the wise and learned.

Paule Yes, you haue read it, if God had giuen you eies to see it : But if your studie had bene principally to aduaunce Gods glorie and benefite his Church, (which you neuer aimed at, but rather preferred vaine glorie and gaine) you shoulde easily haue found it. I pray you therefore, when you come to London, see if you can get these books : the *Ecclesiastical Discipline : a lerned discourse of Ecclesiastical gouernement :* *The Counterpoison : a Sermon on the* 12, *to the romans,* and

M. Cartwri[gh]tes last replye : some of which bookes haue
beene extant this dozen yeres, and yet are none of them
answered, and you shall finde it otherwise.

Diotr If their Lordsh[ips]. were taken away, the credit of
the Gospell would fall to the ground, and men would not
regard it.

Paule Nay, their iurisdiction maketh it not to bee
regarded, for the simplicitie of the gospell, cannot matche
with suche outward pompe, it was of more credit before their
calling was hatched, then euer it was since.

Diotr. I hope neuer to see them ouerthrown, and I thinke
they wil neuer giue ouer their bishoppricks ?

Paul I am of your minde, that they wil neuer giue them
ouer, they haue suche experience of the gaine of them, the
vse of the bagg, preuailed so much with one of the Apostles,
that rather then hee woulde lacke money he would sell Iesus
Christ himselfe.

Diotr. You speak too vnreuerently and vncharitably of
these holy fathers.

Paul Sure I haue so much experience of their impious
dealing, that I canne no better esteeme of them in respecte
of their places, then of the enemies of God, but as they be
men, I wil not ceas[e] to pray for them, that God would open
their eyes, that they may see their sins, and repent, whiche
is the best way to deale charitably with them.

Diotre I pray you tell me why these men be put to
silence, I am sure it is for their notorious misdemeanour.

Paul I will tell you wherefore some of them were put to
silence, one had conference with a bishop about subscription,
and he was restrained for that hee gaue his friende a copie
of his conference, another because he taught that the
Churche of Antichrist was no parte of the Churche of God,
another because his prayers before and after sermons were
too long, and such like.

Diotre A way, it is rather for not obseruing the book of
common prayer, then for any such thing as you speake of.

Paul Indeed many are suppressed therfore but if any
man will giue them their titles and authoritie, they will
giue him leaue to vse his discretion wyth the book, as we
see by experience, for they vse the booke and ceremonies as
bridles to curbe them that kicke at their lordlines, which is
the onely thing that they minde.

Diotrep. Well, I loue not to heare these reuerend fathers so abused, and therefore I praye you talke no more of it, but if it please you, you may depart.

Paul I am contented, onely let me request you this one thing, that for so much as God hath giuen you som[e] lerning, you woulde praye vnto God, to guyde you with his grace, that you abuse it not to your owne destruction, but imploye it to his glory, and the good of his Church

Diotr I thanke you for your good counsel, and so fare you wel, we will talke more in the morning.

Paul With a good will; I praye God our talke may tend to a good end.

Diotr. M[aster]. Demetrius and mine host, howe like you this fellow? is he not a sawcie merchant? to presume thus to speake against those that were preachers before he was borne? but this is the myserie of our nation, that euerye yoong boy will take vpon him to teache the ancient, and to reproue them, for that their greene heades thinke not to bee true?

Pandoch Your Lordship saith verie well, I pray you forget not to vrge him with that in the morning: For it muste needes make him mute.

Demet I promise you, he is a bolde fellowe, it is no maruaile if suche as hee is, doe stand stiffe against vs that be vnlerned, seeing they be so bolde with you, I tell you, he tooke me vp as if I had bin but a kitchin boye, and all because I saide I liued by my money, and was of no other trade, calling me caterpiller, thief, and murtherer, and saide plainly, that he that robbed in Stan-gate-hole, was an honester man then I.

Diotre You must take heed, that you do not oppresse your brother too muche, but as for these fellowes, it is their manner to be so bitter and sharpe, that they do euer with their preaching, more hurte then good.

Demet. I hope you wil course him to morow for it; but I pray you my L[ord]. let me haue a little talke betIween you and me, of a matter that now commeth in my minde; this man that is with you, and went and came in your company, what is he?

Diotrep. To be plaine with you he is a papist.

Demet Papists are enemies to the Queenes religion and lawes; I do therfore much maruail, that he should be put in trust by the byshops?

Diotre The cause is this, he light into the familiaritie of one of our friendes, who confuted a booke called the *Abstract*, and helped him so painefully with reasons out of the Rhemishe Testament, and other such like writers, to confute the Puritans, that he was thought a fit man aboue all other of his religion, to goe with me.

Demetri Why? coulde you not haue had another of your religion, but you muste needes haue a papist your assistant?

Diotr. No no, if I had not had a papist with me, I could neuer haue looked to haue preuailed.

Demetri Why so? I pray you tel me the reason of that.

Diotr Because our dignities and gouernement, commeth wholy and euery part thereof from the Pope, and is ruled and defended by the same canons, wherby his popedome is supported. So that if I had wanted their helpes, I had had none authoritie, eyther from God or man, no helpe either by reason or learning, whereby I coulde haue bene furthered.

Demetri Why did you not rather take some doctour of the Arches, to go with you?

Diotreph That was consulted vppon before I went, but it was not thought meet, because the most of them woulde neuer deale in that lawe at home, but onely because they knowe not else howe to liue, and therfore it was feared that they would not be sufficientlie diligent in a matter that concerneth others. And for the rest (who in deed) be the same men they were in Queen Maries time, we durst not carrie anie of them from home, for none defend our kingdome thorowly but they.

Demet. Me thinks this man should be an vnfit assistant, for he be a right papist, he will labor to erect the popes kingdom, and so crosse you.

Diotr No question but hee did so, and that made for vs, for all be it wee woulde if wee might, of the twaine, keepe rather the protestantes religion with our dignities then the other, yet had we rather change our religion, then to forgo our priuiledges: this I tel you between you and me, but I would haue it go no further?

Demetri Do the old popish doctors stand you in such

gret steed, me think you might haue had learned lawyers for euerye place before this time, and haue turned them out?

Diotre It is true, but we haue retained them of purpose (man) for we can beare, I tel you, with their religion, so that they do beare vp our authoritie; doe you not see likewise, that we haue reserued many popish prists in the ministery, wherof diuers doe yet remaine, which wee haue done vpon special consideration; to wit, lest there should bee too many learned, not one whereof wil stand to vs, saue onely that they either haue, or look to haue better preferment, or liue more easilie then S. Paules Epistles wil allow them.

Demetri I haue bin bolde to trouble your L;ordship`. I will now leaue you for this time, and wil come vnto you in the morninge, to breakfast.

Diotr. You shall be welcome vnto me at all times, for I perceiue you are none of them that fauour the puritans?

Pandoch My L´ord`. your breakfast is ready, wil you haue them come vnto you that were here yesternight.

Diotr I would haue him that taried yesternight so late, for hee is a verye honest gentleman and a quiet, but in any case let not the puritane come vntil breakfast be done, for he is to`o` precise: I must needes be mery, and if he be here, he wil not let to reprooue vs, if we do but fortune to swear at vnawares, so that I shal be a feard of him in euery word I speak

Pandoch Here is but simple cheare this morning, because it is fasting-day.

Diotr M`aster`. Tertullus wil eat no eggs to day: wil you M`aster`. Demetrius?

Demetri Yea by S. Marie, I am a protestant, for I loue to eat flesh on the Friday?

Diotr. It is wel saide, but I pray you, thinke not ill of M`aster`.Tertullus for it, for Saynte Paule hath taught vs, that we that eat, must not iudge them that eat not: for we being strong, must beare with the infirmities of the weake.

Demetri. You promised yester-night, to sende for the puritane, to talke further with him, I pray you do so, for I would haue him taunted thorowly?

Diotrep. By my trothe I had forgotten him, mine host cal him.

Pandoch Here is the gentleman you willed me to call?

Diotr. You are welcome, this Gentleman M[aster]. Demetrius telleth me that you and hee had great controuersie on the way yesterday, and he is very desirous that I might heare your reasons, and giue my iugement of them for his satisfaction.

Paul Sir, I saide nothing to him but the truth out of the word of God, in condemning of vsurie, by which he sayde he liued, and shewed him the horriblenes of the sinne, the inconueniences temporal that come of it in the common-wealth, and the iudgements of God against the practisers thereof.

Diotrep. Vsurie in deed in some sort is vnlawfull, but it seemeth that you dealt not with the man, as meaning to win him, but rather by such sharpenes as might harden him.

Paul Surely my desire was to winne him, and therefore my purpose in reasoning was, to lay open the sinne vnto him, and the cause why I dealt somwhat roundly, was this. He confessed the scriptures that I alleadged, but so cauelled and wrangled against the cleare light therin conteined, that it appeared vnto me his purpose was, not onely to abide an vsurer, but also to iustifie it by the word of God.

Diotre Such chollericke fellowes as you doe mar all, for you cannot deale mildelie and so you trouble the conscience, and disquiet the minde of the weake.

Paul His conscience must be troubled by launcing, before that euer his soul can be cured.

Diotre Then I perceiue you like wel of them that pre[a]ch the law, so much as they do.

Paule Yea, or els shoulde I not like of bringing men vnto Christ, which can neuer be vntil they be humbled by the law, and made pore therby to receue the gospel

Diotrep. Doe you not also like of the preaching of predestination?

Paul Yea, or els should I dislike of preaching the trueth, for it is a part of Gods reuealed will.

Diotreph So do not I in these daies, when there be so manye weake ones, I thinke it to be a very break-necke of all religion.

Paul I haue hearde of freewil men that haue saide so, but I neuer heard [a] man of learning affirme it, but one that was a

byshoppe in a Sermon, but his wordes were no lesse than
blasphemie, and so are yours, and al they that say or think
the same are guiltie of no lesse sinne.

Diotr. Are you a preacher and speake so of these reuerend
fathers, it may be it was your owne ordinary to whom you
are sworne, to giue canonical obedience.

Paul It was the byshop indeed, who vsurped ouer the place
where I dwelt, but I neuer sware him any obedience.

Diotr. Wel, wee are gone from our matter.

Paul And I praye you let vs tarrie a little longer from it,
to consider one thing before we doe returne, whiche the
talking of the byshops bringeth into my head.

Diotr. What is that ?

Paul Surely, that I thinke you are either a B. or els
brought vp in the schoole of a B. and woulde faine bee one, for
you doe vse your selfe verie like, as I haue knowne them do.

Diotre Wherein ?

Paul In this, that whereas we reasoning of vsurie, wherin
your conscience is clear with me, you are contented for the
fauor of him, and for that you like not me, to maintain the
same, and to disgrace the truth, because of the partie that
defendeth it, who is not according to your humor.

Diotrep. You may bee ashamed to speake so of these holy
fathers, I dare saye that none of them euer did so.

Paul If mine eares had not heard it, mine eies not sene,
and mine own person had not felt the experience therof, I
should haue bene of your minde, for I once liked them, and
their verie wicked dealings made me looke into the lawfulnes
of their calling, which I see now to be meere Antichristian,
but shall I tell you one example among many ?

Diotr I am willing to heare you, but I can neuer be
brought to thinke so.

Paule Yet will I tell it you, that you maye thinke of it, I
was accused vnto the B. of suche crimes as were most
slaunderous and false, whervpon I desired him to send for
mine accusers, and see how they could prooue them, that I (if
I were conuicted) might be punnished, or els they might haue
the reward that molesters of the preachers of the Gospell do
deserue : he graunted it me, and appoynted a day, which
being come, rather then I (whom he thought not to fauour
his authoritie) should haue any helpe at his handes, hee made

mee a sleeuelesse aunswere and sent me away. Thus are byshoppes contented to bee bawds vnto all kinde of sinners, rather then they wil any way seeme to further the ministerie of those whom they fauour not, and euen thus doe you : for your hatred vnto my person, maketh you to stand with that monstrous vsurer, but take heede of it, for God will not be mocked, he seeth your dealing, and wil iudge you accordingly, howsoeuer you can pretend the contrarie to the world.

Diotr As for mine owne parte, I passe not what you speake, but let me aske you one question concerning these holy fathers, and that is this, what reason is there that they should do any good in any respect vnto any of you, seing they knowe you to bee professed foes vnto their dignities ?

Paul Because they taking them-selues to be the fathers of the Churche, shoulde haue a regarde to the good cause, and defend it, without respect of persons.

Diotr No sir, I see no reason in that, for aboue all things, they must looke to themselues, without whose authoritie the Gospel would be troden vnder foote : and therefore they may defend no cause nor person further then may stand with their owne safetie.

Paul Suppose that were lawful, what hinderance is this to themselues, to see them that bee common and knowne drunkards, vsurers, adulterers, and profane persons punished, for that they are railers at mee, for teachinge the trueth of religion, and reproouing sharply their godles conuersation.

Diotr Oh you are a simple man, it is great hindrance, for they can doe nothing in defence of you, though it be in matters wherein you and they do agree, but it tendeth to the derogation of their owne estimation, such is the contarietie betwixt your building and theirs.

Paul By that meanes shal we be so wearied with aduersaries, that wee shall neuer haue any hope to doe good, but euen to be constrained to giue ouer the ministerie.

Diotr. I would I might see that once come to passe, we haue labored for it hitherto, and neuer could attaine vnto it, neither will the Churche euer be in quiet vntill you be all turned out.

Paul So thought the Sodomites, that they should neuer be wel, so long as Lot was in their city, but when he was gone, fire from heauen consumed them : but I pray you tel me, if all wee were turned out, how should the people be taught, for it is euident, that none els (almost) maketh a conscience of his duetie that way?

Diotreph You think teaching would fail without you: No sir, teaching woulde bee more regarded then it is.

Paule Shew me how that can be?

Diotr. We would haue none to preache aboue once a moneth, and then should he do it profoundly, and confirme his matter out of the fathers, and humane writers substantially, whereas you taking vpon you to prech three or four times a week, must not only of necessity, handle your matters very rawly, but also breed loathsomnes in the people.

Paul Surely my heart waxeth cold, and my flesh trembleth to heare you speake so monstrously: doth preaching consiste in quoting of doctors, and alleadging of poets and philosophers, in what part of his commission hath a minister warrant so to do: you finde fault with our often preachinge, because your selues cannot so doe, but if you would leaue off your vaine glorie, in hunting after promotion, and your couetousnesse in adding murther vnto theft, I meane liuing to liuing, and betake your selues to studie and prayer, bending your whol[e] endeuor to the glory of God, and edifying of his people, you should see the blessing of God so aboundantly vpon you, that you shold preach foure times euery weeke, with more fruit then you can doe now foure times euery yeere, for while you bee minded as you are. the lords iugement is vpon your gifts, and his curse vpon your labours, that you appeare ridiculous euen vnto children. And whereas you say often preaching cloyeth the people, you shewe your selfe plainly to haue no feelinge in the sweetnes of the worde of God: for it is so delightfull vnto the childe of God, that the more he heareth and readeth it, the more desirous is he to proceed therein, it is the propertie of the vngodly, to whom the word is folishnes to be cloyed with the same.

Diotreph You shal not be my teacher, neyther will I learne at your hands, I know well inough what I haue to do?

Paul I do not speak as a teacher vnto you, but in brotherly loue doe admonishe you, and if you refuse mine, or rather the councell of the holy Ghost vttered by me, you doe but as they doe, whose condition you defend, I pray God forgiue it you, and laye it neither to your nor their charge.

Diotr. They are great moates in your eyes, they know better what to do then you can tel them, they see what is meet for the Church, being ancient graue men of long experience, better then a sorte of yong boyes start vp yesterday.

Paul Though some of vs be but yong, yet al are not so, for we haue som more ancient then they haue any, we haue of al ages and degrees in schools to compare with the best of them, and yet yeares, and humane learning, and experience, must not carrie away the matter, but the euidence of truth in the old and new testament, and as for experience, they haue none, for they were first brought vppe in the vniuersities, then became Deanes, and suche iollie fellowes, and now are made Mitred Lordes, so that they canot tell what it is to traine vp a people to the gospel, and reclaime them from ignorance and sinne, for they neuer stooped so low as to labour therein, but if they had euen my experience, they would sing another song, for before I came into the haruest to worke, I liked their hierarchy wel inough, but when I laid it to my labours to further them, I found that they could not possiblie stand together.

Diotre Did the Gospell euer so flourishe in England as it doth now at this present?

Paul No surely, God be praised for it, and encrease it more and more, but to what end do you speake it?

Diotr To prooue that the authoritie and wise gouernment of the byshops hath had good successe.

Paule I thought so, but it is (if you woulde look into the matter with a single eie) cleane contrarye, for the good that hath bin done, the Lord hath brought it to passe by these men whome you despise, and by that course whiche the bishops were euer enemies vnto.

Diotr. How can you prooue that I pray you, let me hear your reasons that moueth you to think so, for I am perswaded of the cleane contrarie?

Paul It serueth not in this case what you are perswaded of, for a bishoprick hath so blinded your eies, and corrupted your iudgement, that you like nothing but that which agreeth therewithall, but I will shew you my reasons that maketh me of that iudgement, and if you look equallie into the matter, or aske anye indifferent man, you shall see it to bee so.

Diotr. Shewe mee them, for I long to heare them, I am sure they be wise stuffe?

Paul Firste for the men, what congregation, what towne or people is there in this land, that haue bene in the raigne of our soueraign Q Elizabeth, conuerted to the gospel, that those men haue not bene the instruments to perform, whome the bishops haue continuallie persecuted, and for the courses that haue been taken, and which God hath greatly blessed, whiche of them haue not bene ouerturned by the B. and the preachers put to silence, assoone as euer the gospell began to appeare? on the other side, tell me if you be able, of any such effect of the ministerie of a B. or bishoply preacher, in anie place of this land, though it hath bene vninterrupted these twenty years, as you shal see in many places by the other sort, euen in few moneths nowe and then, so that the matter is not onely cleare vnto all that will weigh it in the ballance of equitie, but vnto me, if I had no other reason, it is an euident profe that they take the right way, whose labours the Lord doth so blesse, and contrariwise, the curse of God is on the other, for their indirect dealing.

Diotr Thus you imagin, because you please your selfe in your owne peeuish waies, but tel me who are of your opinion? euen a few puritans like your selfe.

Paul Cal vs as you list, Christ was neuer the worse, for that his enemies called him a seducer and a deceiuer of the people, but I am sure, (all for the moste part that feare God) of euerye degree and calling are of the same minde, sauing those whome you by your subtilties haue bewitched.

Diotr. You wil haue but a fewe then in this lande that feare God, and so you will condemne the rest, which is the manner of you all.

Paul I condemne none, I wishe that not a few, but al (if it were possible) did truely feare God, but I woulde haue you learne of Christe with mee, who maye without disgrace bee your teacher, to try the tree by the fruite, and seeke me out that man which maketh a conscience of sinne, and hath a care to liue as a christian, that is not of the same mind with vs : on the other side, marke what kinde of men they bee, that are the patrons and defenders of the bishops, and you shal see them to be men that make no reckoning of sinne, but haue their wayes fraughted with all impietie, if they bee tried with the touchstone of Gods word.

Diotr. Wel then you confesse yet, that the general sway goeth on our side, and so long as it is so, we care not.

Paul I wil easily grant it, and so haue they from the beginning, and shal to the ending of the world (against al goodnes) but I wil tel you one thing euen of them, that few of them like you in deed.

Diotr. How can these two stande together, many are with vs, and few like of vs, they be meare contrary?

Paul I wil tel you how, the papist is on the B. side, because he can find shilter vnder them to hide his idolatry. The atheist is tooth and naile for them, because by them he inioyeth carnal liberty, the man of most notorious life defendeth them, because he can from them, redeem the corporal punishment of his sins by mony, but non[e] of these like of them indeed. The first, because they keep the possession of the seats of their popishe prelats, the other, because they are so greedie of their courts for money, that euen euerye man crieth shame on them, who then do loue them indeed, and stick to them, onely these three hangbies, that depende vpon them and liue by them, as their chaplins and seruants: the Cananit[e]s (I should say) the canonists: and such ministers as either cannot, or wil not labour in their function, to conuert soules vnto God, so that they doe stinke in the nostrels both of God and man, especially in these three last yeres of their tyrannie, that I do verily hope their sinne is very neere the heigth, and the Lord in mercie will ease vs of them shortly.

Diotre You are a strange fellow, and please your selfe with wonderful persuasions, but I pray you tel me what maketh you saye, they are nowe more hated, seeing that in these last yeeres, the best means haue bene vsed to establish the ministerye in a consent and conformitie vnto them?

Paul Let the meanes be as good as it will, I praise God for the successe of it, howsoeuer the contrary was ment.

Diotre Why praise you God for it, I am sure you neuer liked of it?

Paul The meanes in deede, I neuer liked, neither I thinke, did euer any reasonable man, but it being a brittle wal, daubed with vntempered morter, had that successe that such sandie foundations do deserue.

Diotrep. Why man, what successe had it, I am sure the

greatest part, yea euen of your forwardest men subscribed : and those that did not, are not like to tary in the Church very long.

Paul Wel, sooth vp your selfe in your own perswasion, and brag of the multitude of subscribers, if it were to do againe, hundreds of them would neuer doe it, because they were subtilly circumuented and deceiued (they meaning wel, and tendring the peace of the Church) but (being now sorie for it) wil stand in defence of the cause (I dare say for them) with their brethren, euen vnto death : So that the bish[ops]. haue but their names written : And yet, that (if they would also shew the protestations, and conditions, by which they were induced, and wherof the B[ishops]. made alowance) it would plainly appeare, that either they dealt wickedly to admitte exceptions, if the articles were true, or more vngodly if they wer[e] not, euer to attempt any such matter.

Diotre Tel mee nowe, what is that wherein you seeme to reioyce, as though the issue of it fel on your side ?

Paul It is euen this, that the bish[ops]. straight dealing, made men looke so narrowly into the cause, and to secke the reasons on both sides, for their owne satisfaction, that there are at this day (I am fully perswaded) ten times as many of all degrees, that are fully perswaded of the matters of reformation as were before, so gratious God is vnto his seruants, to make euen their enemies to do them good, and so tender is hee ouer his owne cause and glorie, that he wil make the very meanes intended to oppugne it, bee notable wayes to aduance it.

Diotre. I do not beleeue you, albeit I cannot controlle you in it, because I haue not beene in England of late, but what wil come of it, if it be so ?

Paul Euen the gouernment of the church, by the rules of that Discipline whiche Christe himselfe hath prescribed in his word, which I do perswade my selfe to see before it bee long.

Diotr You woulde bee examined before a iustice and punished, for saying you hope to see an alteration, you cannot be the Q[u]een's[.] friende that thus looke for innouations in the state.

Paule Examine me when you will, and punish mee as God shall giue you leaue, I will be tried to be so far the Q[ueen's].

3 *

friend, as that I wishe so wel vnto her as vnto mine owne
soule, and al that I saye or desire, is not to inuert any thing
in the state that is good, but to haue the corruptions therof
remooued, and her Maiestie more honoured before God and
men, in drawing more neere vnto her God, in aduauncing
the kingdome of his sonne more gloriously within her
dominions.

Diotr These be but feigned words, I do not belieue that
you speake as you thinke?

Paul It is because you measure me by your selfe, who in
deede care neyther for Q[ueen]. Countrie, nor your owne soule,
but for a byshoppricke, but I thanke God in Christ, my
conscience beareth me witnesse, that they bee all verye deare
vnto me.

Diotr. Awaye thou rayling hypocrite, I will talke with
thee no longer, if I catche thee in London, I will make thee
kiss the Clinke for this geare.

Paul In deede the Clynke, Gate-house, White-lyon, and
the fleet, haue bin your onely argumentes whereby you haue
proued your cause these many yeeres, but you shall preuaile
no longer, for your wickednesse is made manifest vnto all
men, which God will shortly repaye into your owne bosomes
seuen folde, but pray to God to giue you repentance, that
those things hapen not vnto you.

Diotr. Pray thou for thy selfe, and care not for mee? I
knowe well inough what I haue to do without thy counsel,
but it is your maner to teach all men?

Tertul Out vpon him, what a fellow is this my Lord : I
neuer hearde such a one in my life,

Diotr I can tell you he gesseth shrewdlie, I perceiue
that our course whiche wee haue taken, and our intent in our
actions, haue bene descried by one means or other.

Tertul My Lorde, it was a thing obserued in the Puritans
at Geneua, and in France, while I was in Rhemes, that we
coulde neuer inuent any practize, for the furtheraunce of the
Catholicke religion, but they knew it often before wee put it
in execution, so that for the moste part, they preuent all our
determinations.

Diotrep. Howsoeuer it be, I am wonderfullie sorie that
they seeme so to triumphe, and that our matters haue no

better successe, it behoueth vs to looke about vs, we will
speed our selues to London, to take some way in hast, least it
be too late, in the meane while, I pray you tel me (for you must
be my counseller when al is done) what way you thinke best to
be taken ?

Tertul I will doe the best I can, but I must first request
one thing of you before I ioyne to helpe you.

Diotrep. What is that ? if it be not vnreasonable, you
may assure your selfe of it, for you know, that I haue neuer
bin strait laced againste you, or anye of your friends.

Tertul I doubt not of it, but how can I haue it before
I aske it of you ? you knowe, that we receiued letters from
England, that there were very hard lawes made this last
Parliament against the Catholiks : this is it therefore I must
request, that you would vse meanes that the rigour of them
be not inforced, for you knowe that wee haue manye both in
Court and countrie, that shall else bee in great daunger.

Diotr I am very well contented to doe so, but what way
shall I take to doe it ?

Tertul Surely, suche a way as shall also make greatly for
your owne cause, and that is this, complaine of the domesticall
foes the puritans, and say, that they be woorse then we, and
that you shall neuer preuaile against vs, vntill firste they
be suppressed, and desire that wee may be let alone for a
time, and that al men would bend their forces against them.

Diotr. This is excellent, I am verye willinge to do this, for
it wil helpe forward our owne cause : nowe go on, and tell
mee what is to be done further ?

Tertul The first thing you must take in hand, must be the
suppression of those preachers in London, and in other
countries, that be of most speciall note, for their forwardnes
against you, and you must do it very wisely : that is, you
may not suppresse them all at once, neyther all of them in a
long time, for you must take heede that the world do not
conceiue opinion of you, to be enemies to the Gospel, for
then haue you no way but to turne wholie vnto vs.

Diotr That will be a verye good waye, but how shal we
haue good matter against them, for their liues are thought to
be very vpright, and they haue learned of late to be more
pollitike then heretofore, for if they speak against any thing
established, they doe it so cunningly, that aduantage cannot
be taken against them by law ?

Tertul Neuer doubt of that, was there euer any man that ment to beat a dogg, but he could easily finde out a staffe to doe it, you muste in this case preferre your safetie before your credite, or the estimation of anye that belongeth vnto you?

Diotr. Yea, but shew me some perticulars, for I promise you, I see not how to doe it?

Tertul You must be sure to let none preach at Paules crosse, but they of whom you haue experience to like well of you, and you muste giue them instructions before hand, that they inuey mightily against the reformation that your aduersaries desire, and there wil one or other of them speake against that, and so you may haue sufficient aduantage against them.

Diotre But these fellowes be verye sharpe to finde a faulte? what and if the matter which our friend preacheth be false, and so the other take occasion to confute it?

Tertul Then must you vrge him to defende that which he hath said, and so shal you haue more occasion to intrappe the aduersarie.

Diotrep. But in so doing, he whome we set on worke shall lose his credit.

Tertul what and if he doe, do you compare his credit with the waight of your byshopricks? there is no comparison?

Diotr You saye true, but what if it shall fall out, that the aduersarie be not blameworthie, neither in matter nor maner?

Tertul If he maintaine the controuersie, it is sufficient cause to put him to silence thogh he haue the better part, for you must maintain the peace of the church

Diotr But this is not all, for how shal we do for the courte, that is the place, whiche aboue all we must fortifie, or els we are gone?

Tertul In deede there is great care to be had of it, and there be many wayes to preuent vs there, but we will doe what we can in it. First you must take heed from time to time, what chaplains be put to the Q[ueen]. seeing they are the teachers of the whole court, namelie, that they be eloquent of toong, and good companions, not too precise in their conuersation.

Diotr. It is verie true, for they may els mar all, I haue hearde some of them speake daungerouslye, euen before her Maiestie.

Tertul Therefore you must take heede, that they be such as can be contented with the course of the worlde, and then if they happen to speake home now and then (as it is a thing incident vnto a rethorician to be girding) the courtiers will neuer regard his wordes, because they see hee walketh not according to that himselfe.

Diotre But I am afraid that the court shal in time come to knowlege by their preaching, and then we are gone.

Tertul Feare not that? I read once in a book made by one of the puritans, that if a man would haue the blessing of God (as he termed it) vpon his hearing, he must submit himselfe to an ordinarie teacher, which thing (I promise you) is some-what: for I see, that the greatest knowlege of their religion, is in those places, and men that haue the same ordinarie teacher : and therefore keep them from anye more preaching, than on euerye Sunday, and that by diuers men, and I warrant you that gappe is stopped for euer.

Diotr. It is something that you say, and I will not forget to looke vnto it, but there is another thing which is greater then that, which is, howe we may keepe the Queene on our side, for I haue often feared her, seeing (there is no question) but she is grounded in the foundation of religion.

Tertul How haue you kept in with her all this while?

Diotr. Marie thus, we haue bene verie careful to take heede who bee admitted to preache before her in the Lent : There was one Deering, that by our neglygence preached once : if he and such as he, had but continued the whol[e] Lent, I am afraide, there would haue bene neuer a Lord Byshop left in England before the next Lent had come againe.

Tertul That I like very well, but that is not all, they wil make books, and it cannot bee but some of them do come to her hands, how will ye do if she like well of them, and the matter of Discipline in them?

Diotr. I promise you I cannot tel, you must helpe vs at that dead lift, or else we are vndone.

Tertul It is an easie matter to remedie, you must when you hear her speake of such things, make her beleeue that al is wel, and that the drift of these men is not seene, for they woulde haue no Magistrate, and so would pul downe Kinges and Princes, and this wil be sure to preuaile, and make them to bee esteemed the vilest men aliue.

Diotr. Howe can I tell her that all is well, when I haue beene constrained to tell diuers preachers, that haue so sore vrged me with the text, that I could wish things were amended: but the Q[ueen]. wil not at any hand?

Tertul Surely, you are a very simple man, my Lord, (as though) the Queene heares what you saye to them, or they, what you saye to the Queene, you must still continue that course of excusing all thinges to her, for shee beleeueth that you are learned, and lay all the blame when you talke with them on her, (for you cannot ouerthrow them by Scripture) and so you shall not onelye keepe the Q[ueen]. on your side: but also make the preachers haue a tollerable opinion of you, that you would haue some things refourmed if it lay in you.

Diotr. That is a notable way, I will alwaies obserue and practise that, but there be many noble men, counsellors, and great courtiers, that seeme to like wel of our aduersaries: how shall we do to retayne them, or to bridle them that are gone from vs?

Tertul That wil be somewhat hard to doe: yet the best counsell I can see meete to be taken, is this: you must shewe your selues very affectionate vnto those that desire glorie and estimation, you must winke at the vices of all of them whatsoeuer they be, and not reproue them, much lesse correct them; and those of them that bee needie, you must haue them to beg the Byshoppricks, Deanries, and such great places, and let them that shall haue them pay wel for them. So shall you not onelye haue them beholding vnto you for a benefitte, but keepe them still on your side, in hope to haue the like bootie another time.

Diotr. This is very well, and shal bee alwaies obserued: but there is yet an other thing, I heard of late, that there be verie manye gentlemen and gentlewomen in the Court, that like vs not, and it hath often times bene, that kings and princes, haue beene induced by information of meane menne, to doe that which greate counsellours coulde not beat into their heads, how shall we do to stay the mischiefe that may come of these?

Tertul Easilie, you must consider that they be of two sorts: either they be such as bee highly in fauour, or they bee common courtiers, if they bee of the former sort, You

must when you haue o[p]portunity to speake to her, tel her,
that shee must take heede of such, and such persons : for
though they be verie wise and discreet (bicause you must not
dyslike anye that shee liketh) yet are they (being of a good
nature) deceiued, by the fair pretence of Puritans, and for the
other you may say they do great harm, by reason of their
countenaunce in the court, with fauoring the Puritanes, so
that it shall come to passe, by these informations, that the
Queene shall not onely reiect their speeches, (if they vse any
against you) but also take them vp roundly, that they shall
not dare to speake any more.

   Diotr. This pleaseth mee at the very heart, but how shall
we doe to be sure at the Counsell table, for they are wise,
and manye of them like vs but from the teeth outwarde, and
we haue receiued many a foyle there ?

   Tertul That is euen the hardest of all : I know not in the
whole world any way but one.

   Diotr. Tell me that one, for if once I knowe it, we will
say wel to it, but we wil bring it to passe ?

   Tertul This is it, in King Edwardes dayes ther wer[e] Bb.
of the counsel: now if you could get (though it were but
one) to be a counseller, then might he very wel, whensoeuer
any matter of complaynt came, tell the Lords it pertained to
ecclesiasticall iurisdiction, and he and his brethren woulde
heere it at large : so might he stop their mouthes quickly,
and then hee might for fashions sake, heare the cause, but
sende the plantifes away with a flea in their eare.   And thus
very quickly would all complaintes to the counsell cease.

   Diotr. Oh moste notable deuice, all our friends in England
shal fayle vs, but we will haue this take place : there is yet
another thing that must bee helped, and that is the vniuersities,
for they haue great priuiledges, and puritanes starte vp there
euery day.

   Tertul So there will do some do what you can, vnlesse
you haue fire and fagotte, (which weapon of ours, you only
lack, and none else) the best course that I knowe to be taken
is this, let no Colledge chuse his owne head, but let him haue
a Mandamus, procured from the Queene, and see that he be
such a one as hath bene a non-resident before, and let him
haue diuers liuings : and so that will draw with it formalitie.
Let him be the Q[ueen's]. chapline, or at the least brought nowe

and then to preache in the Lent, and that will so set him a
gog for a Bishoppricke, that you shalbe sure he wil suppresse
your aduersaries as they arise, and let the heades of the
houses be admonnished from time to time, that they chuse
none to be fellowes that be puritans, but such as like the
state, and for the more assurance, let them be vrged to
subscribe, yea, to sweare to your authoritie, before they be
admitted.

Diotrep. Shall we go to Cambridge, and see this put in
execution as we go ?

Tertul Nay soft, be sure of the court, before you enterprise
any other where, least you marre all.

Diotr. You say very well : nowe how shall we doe for the
parsons and vickers, of the countrie that like vs not ?

Tertul I promise you, those that be in alreadie, will say
harde vnto you, and those that bee to come also, if they will
subscribe to the articles, so far as they concerne faith and
sacraments, the statute law fauors them too much.

Diotr But haue we no helpe by the canon lawe ?

Tertul Yes, there is helpe inough in the canon law, if they
will take it : but I will tell you one thing in your eare, which
I would not for a thousand pounds were knowne abroad, and
that is this : if the statute made in the 28. of H. oct. cap. 19
and the reuiuing of it in the 1. of Elizabeth, cap. 1. were
thorowly sifted, I am afraid, not any cannon lawe would
be found good law in England, and so what woulde become
of you, and your aucthoritie ? but I knowe to whome I do
speake it.

Diotr What shall we doe then ?

Tertul You must set a good face vpon the matter, and
pretend law, both statute, and cannon, especially cannon,
bicause they know not that, then depriue them of their
liuings, which if they (though they know you do them wrong)
could remedie by law, yet are not their purses so wel filled
as yours, and so lack of liuing wil make them to yeeld at
length, as we see it hath done many.

Diotr. But may we not well suppresse them, for not vsing
the surplice, and book of common prayer in all points ?

Tertul I tell you there is no law in England to hurt them,
for any thing that they haue done concerning the surplice,
the Iudges hauing bene set on by you and vs, haue indited

them for it, but it is more then they can warraunt by lawe, and as for the booke it is cleare, that the strickte keeping of it was meant against vs, but wee thanke you for turning the edge to them from vs. Summum ius, must be your best help in this case, and looke that you practize it continuallie.

Diotrep. This will do very wel, how shal we do to keep the Ministerie from too much knowledge, for that must bee doone, though we pretend the contrary?

Tertul In deede, it is a thing that you must looke narrowlye vnto, and therefore take heed aboue al things, that the exercises of prophesie come not vp again, for you know what harme they did vnto you in euery place where they were kept, and especiallie where men were moderators therin, that had bene beyond the seas, to see the practise of them at Geneua, and you must beware of the exercises that ministers haue at their meetings : for you knowe, that in Leicester-shire, they furthered knowledge greatly.

Diotre But how shall we do with this, the exercise of prophesie is expresly set down in the 14. of the 1. to the Cor. and it is knowne that they whome you and we set on worke to gette it forbidden, confessed since that they knewe it not, but tooke it to be foretelling of things to come, and not expounding of the scriptures.

Tertul You must answere it as you do the rest of their reformation, the particulars whereof are expressed in the newe Testament : namely, that they were things onely for that time, and for them that helped you, what if they confessed their ignoraunce? you must stil accuse their exercises to bee vnlawful assemblies, and conuenticles to breed sectes and schismes, and your authoritie wil beare you out in al this and more to o .

Diotr. But what shall wee doe to make the worlde beleeue we would haue the ministery learned ?

Tertul Make them first ministers, and then set them too schoole, enioyning them to get som[e] part of M[aster]. Nowels Catechism, or of Bullingers Decades by heart, and so you shall seeme to desire a learned ministerie, as wel as these reformers.

Diotr. Wee wil not faile to put this also in practize, is there anye more that you knowe, that may serue our turnes, for the further establishment of our dignities ?

Tertul No nothing of any great waight, but it may be referred to some one of these pointes, but the particulars of euerye braunche are many, which your owne wisedome may easily looke vnto.

Diotr Then let vs go, for I long vntil I do set these things abroach.

Tertul Yet I pray you remember to do somthing for vs poore Catholikes, seeinge you stande by our helpe especially.

Diotr. Great reason we should doe so, or els were wee vngrateful creatures, but you must deuise what must be done?

Tertul You knowe that some of vs be in prison, and others abroad, for those that are restrained, I pray you that they may haue the libertie of the prison, and their friendes to come too them, and when anye of them come before you, that you would deale fauourably with vs.

Diotr Your request is verye reasonable, for the first you shal see that your friendes shal haue the best chambers in euerye prison, and when anye puritane falleth into our handes, you shal see him haue the most stincking place that can bee found. Now when any of you, yea if you your self com[e] before vs, you must be content to let vs rayle on you, and call you traitors, and threaten you greuously, but you shalbe sure you shall sustaine small harme, if you receiue any, you must impute it to the times and not to vs.

Tertul I thanke your Lordship, let vs now be going, for we haue tarried too long in our lodging this morning.

Diotre Hee neuer tarrieth too long that is wel imployed, as we haue beene, it was the best morning that euer I spent.

Demet. How now mine host, what say you to these ioly fellowes, had not they notable talke?

Pandoch Yes sir, I haue learned of them, that that will do me good I hope.

Demet What is that?

Pandoch I haue learned howe to course our preacher, and hee shall be sure of it, and though it cost mee the price of a tunne of wine.

Demetri Why, what doth he that deserueth coursing?

Pandoch What? He setteth men together by the eares, the towne was neuer at quiet since he came, he teacheth

such doctrine as some doo like, and some not, and so they
fall at variance.

Demetri I pray you tell me some particulars of the worst
of all.

Pandoch This for one : our towne standeth on vittelling,
because it is a thorow-fare, and he preacheth against good
fellowship (which hee calleth drunkennesse) and against
playing at cardes and tables, wherein, if he might haue his
wil, I and my neighbors might go on begging within one
twelue-moneths, and he hath so preuailed. that I take not so
much by foure poundes in a weeke, as I was woont to doe :
yea I haue had ten shillings of one man in a weeke for
drincke onelie, that will nowe scarce spend three, but I will
looke vnto him.

Demetri Well mine host, deceiue not your selfe, I
perceiue that you and I are in a wrong boxe, you are an enimy
to the Preacher, because he speaketh against your vnlawfull
gaine, and so was I yesterday with him that tooke the same
course to amend me : and I thought he had spoken falsly,
because he was a Puritan : and when I came to heare my
matter debated, the bishop disallowed my course, and yet
tooke my parte. And why ? Because I might defend him
in his vnlawfull calling. But I see their iugling wel inough,
and if the manne, with whome I was so offended be not gone,
I will talke further with him, for I perceiue that hee meant
better vnto me than they did.

Pandoch I perceiue we shall haue a Puritan of you, if
you would so faine speake with him, he is but newe gone out
at the gate, you may ride after him : but as for our Preacher,
I will in hand with him, because I cannot tel howe I shall
else gaine my liuing, and maintain my selfe as heeretofore I
haue doone.

Dixi.

THE CONCLVSION.

Rethren, ye see by lamentable experience, howe iniuriouslie the church of G O D in England is dealte withall, by taking away, and stopping the mouths of their faithful teachers, and by thrusting vppon vs vnlearned and vnsufficient menne, which neither haue wil nor abilitie, with wholsome barking to driue away the woolfe, but contrariwise dooth giue priuie encouragement vnto the enemie, to continue in his wickednesse, whereby the church of God is assailed most dangerouslie: and Sathan doth not ceace by al meanes possible, to ouerthrow that good worke which is begunne in England: and therefore it behooueth vs brethren, to looke about vs, and not to suffer the enemie to growe so strong against vs, if by anie meanes wee may let and hinder his wicked enterprises. And now, my brethren, what is to bee done on our partes? Surelie I am one of the simplest of a thousand, to giue aduise to proceede in any good course in so waightie a matter. But this, in my iudgement were a good waye, euen to ioyne our selues together, so manie as feare G O D, and to frame our moste humble supplication vnto her Highnesse, shewing vnto her Maiestie the greate dammage and losse that the Churche dooth sustayne, for that they can not haue the voyces of their faithfull pastors, which haue diligently, and with great paines labored to draw men backe from superstition, and the false worship of God, vnto the true and sincere worship of his maiestie, and laying downe before vs most purely, the doctrine of the Scriptures, to the end, that we should know what wee ought to doe, and what to leaue vndoone, leading vs, as it were, euen by the hand, vnto the true worship of God, and our loyall dutie vnto her Maiestie, and al her officers. And these men (we can not tel by what meanes) are letted and stopped

from dooing those notable dueties of their calling, and are
not permitted to speake anie more vnto vs in the name of
the Lord, whereby we hir poore subiects sustaine great dearth
and scarcitie, euen of the foode of our soules. Therefore wee
her loial subiects, most humbly do entreate her highnesse,
that shee woulde looke vpon the affliction of the poore Churche,
and let vs haue our true teachers restored vnto vs againe.
And so we her subiects should yeeld continual thanks vnto
her highnesse, praying vnto God alwayes for her prosperitie.
And (our brethren) if this way shall be thought good, when
there shalbe some aduice taken vpon it. Then to choose out
some fitt man that can indite and frame our supplication, one
that feareth God, that hath a feelinge of this plague in his
hearte (as the Scripture speaketh) I meane of the want and
lacke of these good preachers.

And this beeing doone, then to appoint other godly and
honest men, to present our supplication, two or three, as it
shall bee thought good vnto you, and the rest to ayd them
with money, or in what other daunger may fal out : so that
they present it in the name of the whole congregation, or
otherwise, if it shalbe thought good. First to moue our sute
vnto some of the Byshops, as Winchester or Salisburie, or
both, or anie other that you shall thinke good : I beseech you
let vs not sit stil, when wee are touched so neer, but as those
good men haue ventured their libertie and liuing for our
good : so let vs take some paines for them, to aduenture some
daunger of reproofe, or what else maye fall out.

Better is the day of death (saith Salomon) then the day of
birth, man that is borne of a woman, liueth but a short time,
and is replenished with many miseries, but happie are the
dead, that die in the Lord.

Man is borne of woman in trauell, to liue in miserie, man
through Christe, doth die in ioy, and liue in felicitie. He is
borne to die, and dieth to liue. Straight as hee commeth

into the worlde, with cries, hee vttereth his miserable estate,
straight as he departeth, with songs he praiseth God for euer.
Scarce yet in his cradle, three deadlie enemies assault him :
after death no aduersary can anoy him : whilest hee is here,
hee displeaseth God : when he is dead, he fulfilleth his will.
In this life, here he dieth thorow sinne, in the life to come,
he liueth in righteousnes, thorowe many tribulations in earth,
he is still purged : with ioy vnspeakable in heauen, is he
made pure for euer : here hee dieth euerie howre, there hee
liueth continuallye : heere is sinne, there is righteousnesse :
heere is time, there is eternitie : heere is hatred, there is
loue : heere is paine, there is pleasure : heere is miserie,
there is felicitie : heere is corruption, there is immortalitie :
here we see vanity, there shall wee behold the maiestie
of God, with triumphant and vnspeakable ioye in glorie
euerlasting.

Seeke therefore the things that are aboue, where Christ
sitteth on the right hand of God the father, to whom
with the sonne and the holie ghost, be al
honour and glorie, worlde
without ende
Amen.

www.ingramcontent.com/pod-product-compliance
Lightning Source LLC
Chambersburg PA
CBHW021437090426
42739CB00009B/1526